Last Minutes

AF354953

Lynn Brown

Last Minutes © 2022 Lynn Brown

All rights reserved.

No part of this publication may be reproduced, stored in a retrieval system, or transmitted, in any form or by any means, electronic, mechanical, photocopying, recording or otherwise, without the prior written permission of the presenters.

Lynn Brown asserts the moral right to be identified as author of this work.

Presentation by *BookLeaf Publishing*

Web: www.bookleafpub.com

E-mail: info@bookleafpub.com

ISBN: 978-93-95890-12-0

First edition 2022

For Freya and Maya

Her Wellies

Her wellies are for running, jumping and
splashing.
For slipping in playgrounds and breaking
her teeth.

They go with her joggers, her dresses and tights.
She won't be told otherwise
but you can try if you like.

Her wellies stomp over flowers, through puddles
and fields.
For rainy days and dry days and all in between.

They skip up to school and fly down the road.
She won't take them off, they're her favourite
you know.

So many footprints they've already left, and so
many more they have yet to go.

The Big Bang

The world they say begun
with a loud almighty bang
I can understand their reasoning now,
having seen one in the making.

For surely there's no other way to describe,
the beginning of the world you made me.
A seismic shift, a frightening plunge, completely
unfamiliar.

Then the world I knew had gone completely;
replaced with something new.
In place of doubt and fear and worry
you put safety, hope and joy.

And if the old world tries to pull me back,
I just think and smile.
Your laugh, your warmth, you curls and cuddles,
keep my feet both firmly planted.

Man on the Moon

The man on the moon is eating his cheese,
counting the stars around him.

Between them and the sun, who he adores just as
much, he doesn't feel very important.

For he does not know, that from far down below,
it is him who is shining the brightest.

Made with Love

Little fingers curl
through each individual stitch,
you hug the blanket close
and smile just a smidge.

Made with such tender care,
providing comfort and protection.
It's no wonder you sleep so sound,
wrapped up in its affection.

Dear Freya

A little unexpected,
Our lives you have upended.

A little hand to hold,
Worth more than any gold.

A little shock, quickly overcome,
With the love of getting to be your mum.

A little more you grow and grow,
Oh how I wish time would slow.

A little love seeps every day,
Deep down into my soul to lay.

A little bit longer, I plead and I plead
That'll you'll still need me, just a little.

Mira

Softly purring in the night or yowling to your
hearts delight.
Licking paws, scratching your claws, trying to
squeeze into drawers.

Stretching your limbs and chasing strings.
Curling up at my feet, finding yourself a comfy
seat.

A little thing you are for sure, but I know you
have a heart so pure.

Dear Maya

Life moves fast and slow,
While every day I watch you grow.
Both at the same time,
anticipation and loss combine.

The days gone past I mourn
And from my first born,
I know
To cling to the memories before they go.

Time is precious and cruel
But its tick cannot be overruled.
No matter how hard we wish,
Nothing can remain just like this.

I look forward to all things to come.
To be all you deserve in a mum.
And through al the dark and roughest nights
We'll live for life's great delights.

So please remember not to live too long
outside of the present where you belong.
And know that with every tick,
Time wont allow our love to shrink.

My Grandad

A man you have not met,
quite like this man I'll bet.

There's nothing he cannot fix,
whether its wood, paper or brick.
And if he does not know it yet,
He'll learn it, don't you fret.

For lets not forget his brain
which makes others look quite plain.
Attention to detail you must have noticed,
I've never seen someone quite so focused.

He has a pirates treasure,
stroll through it at your leisure.
Radios, trains and old styled ploughs,
will just begin you on your browse.

And musically inclined he is,
though he'll ask you to be his singers.
I know an old lady who swallowed a fly,
will always make the night sail by.

But best of all his heart of gold,
that loves us all tenfold.

A man you have not met,
quite like this man, I'll bet.

A fairies dream

I used to dream of a world
so very far away,
where fairies dance, dragons fly and all the
pixies play.

But I've discovered it's but a childhood dream,
with too much hope and wonder.
No realities to consider.

As the fairy dance is deadly, the dragon fire
quite real.
And pixies speak in riddles with hidden truths
you don't want to feel.

And now I wonder why I dreamed at all
when it's become quite clear,
that childhood was the dream,
with the world not so surreal

Sailing ship

The slightest look or touch or gasp
sent tremors down my spine.
But they ricocheted and found my heart
then right down to my soul.
How quickly I fell; I cannot grasp.

And soon I was only whole with you,
you seeped into every thought.
But life has troubles, toils and pains
And our wants and needs were different.
Looks could easily be those of disdain
and not always quite so considerate.

But learning fast we steered this ship
Through currents, winds and downpours.
Rewarded we were for our strong grip
with a life full of splendours.

And what started from a shaky, kindled kiss,
has emerged a blissful world in which we can
always reminisce.

Cloud jumpers

Have you seen the cloud jumpers,
way up in the sky?
I wonder if they fly?

Or perhaps they start on mountain tops or on a
tower? And simply jump up higher…

Do you think they are there just for fun?
Or on a special mission?

Are they protecting us from threats above?
Or think we're something to get rid of?

Either way I'd join them, and jump through any
cloud,
Just to feel a little lighter and not hear
everything so loud.

Dear Sean

You've been through so many changes
In not so very many ages.
Physically and mentally,
Emotionally too.

From ashes we have risen,
Freed from your own prison.
And looking at you now
Just fills me up with pride.

But I do feel rather lacking,
Like I've been caught slacking.
When I see the work you've done
And the accomplishments achieved.

I am so very grateful for everything's that's
passed,
It's brought us to this very spot, I'm sure we
have been blessed.
Can you see how far you've come and taken all
your credit?

I hope your love has grown for me
like mine has grown, you see
I cannot live without you now,
You're the very air I breathe.

What's a sister for?

15

Stealing shirts, switching skirts,
singing in the rain.

Secret sharing, sports day skiving,
staring people down.

Snowman sculpting, screaming, shouting,
swimming in the sea.

Soothing sounds, spending pounds
A best friend for life you'll see.

Tick Tock

The mouse runs round the clock
Scurry scurry, tick tock

Endless tasks to fill the day
No time to do as you may
Scurry scurry, tick tock

Stress rising as you chase
the minutes at their fastest pace
Scurry scurry, tick tock

Wondering where the hours have gone
When you haven't even mowed the lawn
Scurry scurry, tick tock

Washing folded, teas been made
Just the kids bedroom left to raid
Scurry scurry, tick tock

And as you finally feel you've won,
That insufferable clock again strikes one
Scurry scurry, tick tock

The mouse runs round the clock
Scurry scurry, tick tock

Twinkle Twinkle

Autumn has been left behind;
a chill creeps through the wind.
Crisping up the autumn leaves
as the water starts to freeze.

The nights close in around us
while frosts cling to the truss.
Breath hangs in the air like smoke,
You're wrapping in your warmest cloak.

A thousand things the darkness brings just look
in the sky.
As while the sun is further gone
the stars are bright till dawn.

And the peace the constellations bring
Won't make you wait for spring.
Those cool and calm and crispy nights
Make winter one of life's delights.

Piries Pies

You won't get a pie like Piries
they simply are the best
Steak and gravy, macaroni
You must put them to the test.

World winning scotch
in pinched pastries,
peppered to perfection.
A favourite for all the parties.

Handmade with extra special care
to ensure they leave you wanting more.
So get yourself a Piries Pie
and sink your teeth into the delicious core.

Crazy Book Lady

Come and take a look
At my favourite books.
I've organised them on the shelves
Feel free to help yourselves.

A romance, mystery
plain old fantasy;
Your more than welcome to get lost
in a world where you'll be engrossed.

Just be careful with the pages fine
And the fragile paper spine.
These books are my prized possessions
or maybe they're classed as obsessions.

Magic or Science

Magic or science you tell me,
There is no difference I can see.
This tiny little flower can create
a whole new plant, just you wait.

And multiverses may be real
All those stars just seems surreal.
Dinosaurs once walked this earth,
Then there's the miracle of birth.

Every topic you consider
Holds nothing but wonder
So science or magic you tell me,
There is no difference I can see.

www.ingramcontent.com/pod-product-compliance
Lightning Source LLC
La Vergne TN
LVHW021350200726

843509LV00014B/2763